Toccata and Fugue with Harp

Nature versus Nurture?

Reflections on growing up in the post war era, viewed through a lens of music and colour.

First published 2024 by The Hedgehog Poetry Press,

5 Coppack House, Churchill Avenue, Clevedon. BS21 6QW

www.hedgehogpress.co.uk

ISBN: 978-1-916830-32-5

Toccata and Fugue with Harp

by

Margaret Royall

Dedicated to my newly rediscovered family who have brought such joy into my life: Ann Corringham, Elizabeth Corringham & partner Paul and the Kirsopps, Janet, John and Hannah.

Thank you for welcoming me into your fold.

PROLOGUE

Duetting with Life

He tells me:

Place the polished curves
gently beneath your dimpled chin;
now let your nimble fingers flirt
with the eager well-tuned strings.

Tilt your head, flick back your
flowing mane of chestnut curls,
pick up your resined bow, balance
it lightly in your sensitive hand

and let your music sing out:
pure purring notes of unchained ecstasy
rising up within you, chaste and unblemished
like a fresh spring dawn.

I am that violin, your Muse,
your heart's delight and desire,
making music with you, responding
to the plea of the plaintive strings;

strong chords of passion in crescendo,
vibrating, echoing through time and space;
now gentle pizzicato, now with the timbre
of a D sharp minor tryst.

Together we fashion new melodies,
broadcast symphonies to the world,
hearts brimming over with pride
as the duet seals our lovers' knot.

Contents

PART ONE: TOCCATA

The musical cadences of my early years

Philip Larkin wrote:

'They fuck you up, your mum and dad.
They may not mean to, but they do.
They fill you with the faults they had
And add some extra, just for you.'

MY CHILDHOOD IN CONTEXT

Religion   what should I say?
a force for good or root cause of evil?

For a '50s child church and school were dominant.
We had no television, no fridge, no washing machine,
no internet or social media; we made our own entertainment,
read books, pursued hobbies, played freely outdoors.

Parental influence was strong, discipline usually strict;
rebellion was quashed as soon as it reared its ugly head.

In schools corporal punishment was rife.
There were vindictive teachers, who enjoyed
humiliating us, dispensing severe beatings.

Children were more easily controlled,
career choices were narrower, especially for women.

It was into this period of social history that I was born,
a post-war child in a loving family at a time of austerity
and food rationing, just prior to the launch of the NHS.

My parents had lived through two World Wars,
were eager to give me the best start in life.
They did it with love, in the only way they knew how.
The doctrines of the Methodist church had served them both well.

But sometimes, though unaware of it,
they lived their lives vicariously through me -
and that was stressful. I was their everything.
At times I felt like a misfit, a stranger
looking in on the world from the sidelines.
I felt different.

BLACKCURRANT WINE

Inspired by Ruth Stone's 'Pokeberries'

I started out on the chilly Lincolnshire coast
with my Granddad's thriving tomato plants
and my Nanna Kate's country superstitions.
Teatime meant dripping on toast or boiled egg.
My Mum would polish the red linoleum till it shone .
She married my Dad, her childhood sweetheart,
who adored her, despite her blind eye and thick glasses.
They went to Southport on honeymoon and
nearly drowned in a yacht they took to sea.
My parents were devout Methodists, who played
hymns on our old piano and were tee-total.
My dad preached Sunday sermons in far-flung chapels
where communion wine was blackcurrant - alcohol free.
My whole upbringing was based on the Methodist faith,
I couldn't escape it.
And there were many factors complicating my life,
until a new man started work with me and I ran away
with him, living at first in a holiday camp chalet.
I stuck with him despite his wandering eye
and penchant for pretty women with red lipstick.
We were welded like super glue, like the stuff
my uncle once glued his fingers to the hen coop with.
But come what may, no one could completely shake
religion out of me, not my Granddad nor my Nanna Kate
nor my parents, who didn't just attend chapel on Sundays,
they haunted it – along with the temperance wine!

PROHIBITION

The rules were always very clear,
the don'ts outweighed the do's
The credo we were given went thus:

No working on Sundays
No knitting, sewing, ironing, cleaning gardening
No riding on a bus on a Sunday
No going in a shop on a Sunday
No gambling, no betting, no games of chance   ever
No going to horse-racing, greyhound racing or the like.
No drinking alcohol   ever   hence
No going in a pub or bar   ever
No purchasing liquor in the offie
No missing the Sunday service at chapel
No wearing trousers for women
No unnecessary self-adornment
No living beyond your means
No purchasing on the 'never never'
No sex before marriage
No divorce
No lending money, no borrowing money
No answering back your elders or betters
No lying, no cheating, no stealing!

In fact more prohibition than permission!

NANNY BUTTLE SINGS A HYMN TO THE TUNE CWM RHONDDA

Bread of Heaven, bread of Heaven
feed me till I want no more....

She sang, oh how she sang!

Church and God the crutches
on which she leaned; blind faith
reflected in impromptu renditions
of her beloved Cwm Rhondda.

That all-pervading scent of Pears soap
caught in her aura, the pungent kick of
Amami setting lotion from Friday night's
shampoo and set; loose overalls baggy across
shrivelled breasts that mourned the pert nipples
of a lost youth.

A simple countrywoman   happy in her skin,
superstitious   moulded from local clay
from daisy chains   from May Day revelries
Harvest suppers   first communion
sunsets that gobbled up the sky.

Her voice crescendoed verse on verse,
adopting the bravado of an autumn robin
facing an unknown winter, singing full-throated.

We were transported to the Welsh valleys:
to winding towers   slag heaps   poverty
Sunday-school girls with ribboned ringlets,
young men with pit-black hair and chapel-ready vibrato,
grannies with street-map faces pointing the way to Zion.

Yet sadly Nanna had no memory of yesterday's
dinner or the home visit from Doctor Brown,
bearing confirmation of senile dementia.

But ask her to scrub the fireplace, clean out
the grate and she was instantly nine years old again,
singing the old familiar hymns with her mum.

Nanny had never been to Wales, but in the music
of the valleys she found respite from a world of confusion...

Bread of Heaven, bread of Heaven
feed me till I want no more...

ASTROPHOBIA

An irrational fear of thunderstorms

When thunderstorms loomed
my Nan would shake with terror;
like a hare, poised on hind legs,
gathering her voluminous aprons to her body,
preparing to run and hide.

She was a country lass,
raised in a close-knit community,
where clouds were nature's soothsayers,
casting omens of good or bad fortune.
At the merest hint of a storm she would quake,
'Looking rare and black ower bull's mother's noo!' *
she would mutter to herself.

Our attempts to demystify thunderstorms failed:
'What a load of kilter and rammel !* Talking like Frim Folks!'*
She scoffed at us, fleeing into hiding at the first clap of thunder,
emerging only when the storm had been drawn out to sea.

*Looking rare and black ower bull's mother's noo = it's looking very grey and dark and bad
weather is coming (a Lincolnshire dialect expression)
* what a load of kilter and rammel = what utter rubbish
* Frim Folks = non Lincolnshire natives

GRANDMA BROWNING'S PRECIOUS SECRETS

Inside a drawer in Grandma's house I found
A precious box with tokens from a tryst,
Her secret notebook, delicately bound.

Victorian love chains, beautifully wound
A lock of hair her husband often kissed
Inside a drawer in Grandma's house I found.

My heart stood still, I dared not make a sound
Exploring these sweet memories of bliss,
Her secret notebook, delicately bound.

A photo of her seated on the ground,
Hair flowing free in strands of golden mist
Inside a drawer in Grandma's house I found.

Two hearts in decoupage on Cupid's mound
With spidery writing, hard to catch the gist...
Her secret notebook, delicately bound.

I sensed that love was swirling all around
Enchanted by this unexpected gift -
Inside a drawer in Grandma's house I found
Her secret notebook delicately bound.

VISITING MY GREAT AUNTS IN LOUTH

A Victorian terrace, frozen in time;
cobwebbed faces with monochrome lives,
slaving long hours at factory benches.

Conformity hidden behind tight-lipped smiles,
ungodly thoughts erased from the bare walls
of the Wesleyan chapel down the lane,
keeping the god-fearing tightly in check.

A two-up-two-down museum
dusted with immortality;
harsh conditions etched on stooped bodies,
faces un-powdered, necks unadorned,
a diet of abstinence and pease pottage
from a bubbling cauldron of propriety.

Mahogany table and chest in best parlour
weighed down by the burden of time:
carved puzzles, tubs of spills, nests of dolls
whittled by idle hands in slack times.
Piano with bent candelabra, accompanying
the obligatory Sunday night hymn-singing –
Guide me, o Thou great Jehovah...

Great Aunt Nellie, cocooned in wool shawls
on her three-legged stool by the hearth,
duetting with her sister Jessie Lucy, arriving
back from the spring with slopping pail.

Out in the yard a wooden privy with thunder-box,
Aunt Sarah's sacking coat, limp on its peg,
offering warmth to urgent visitors.....

Bedlinen, starched to within an inch of its life,
a horsehair mattress with gaping chasms,
huge four-poster drapes concealing
porcelain chamber pots, yellowed with age,

This was an Alice-in-Wonderland place
for me, a wide-eyed slip of a girl,
escaping the ties of parental repression.

PAYING THE COAL BILL IN THE 1940S

My mother insisted it wasn't far,
repeated that same white lie every time.
My tiny feet in their Clark's brown sandals
eager to keep pace with her nylon-stockinged stride.

The number six bus would have taken us there -
a tuppenny ride for mum, free for me.
But apparently God had given us feet to walk with,
so we walked – a huge challenge for a three-year-old.

The coal office was by the railway line.
I loathed the sudden hiss of steam as trains pulled out of
the station, gathering speed, snorting past the office.
To me the engine was a man-eating beast...*the train lion!*

The clerk took out a black ledger, entered columns
of figures with a fountain pen.
I still see his bold strokes, how his lunettes slipped down
his pointed nose, how he peered at me over the top,
usually commenting on my patience.

At least the walk home was less tiring.
We stopped off at Nanny Kate's, bought Walls' ice-cream
from the shop next door with its array of goods,
ranging from Eno's liver salts to Bovril and Spangles.

Once back home we toasted crumpets over the fire, ate them
with lashings of strawberry jam and Mum's home-made treats:
maids of honour, baked strictly according to Mrs Beeton's recipe...
But I usually fell asleep at the table, exhausted by the walk.

MY MOTHER SHOWED HER LOVE IN STRANGE WAYS

My mother ignored my pleas to help her bake.
I had to stand beside her, watching quietly.

The default message coming across was simply
"Children should watch and learn. Don't ask!"

Excuses varied:'You'd make too much mess,'
or even 'I'm in a hurry. It would take too long.'

It was the same thing with my hair.
As a child she forced me to have dreadful perms,
a shaming curly frizz.

She insisted on washing my hair for me
until I was fifteen!
I resented this suppression of independence,
felt babied by her.

One day she went shopping with a friend, so I
washed my hair in the kitchen sink with Fairy Liquid,

dried it straight with the hairdryer, just as my friends did.
Her reaction was pure anger; she spat fire and brimstone.

'How dare you? What were you thinking?
Look at the mess !'

I learned submission, felt belittled, stripped of respect
that other mothers gave their daughters.

She did it out of love, I know that now, out of fear
I might stray from the Methodist path, (Heaven forbid!)
or make a fool of myself...

It was always about appearances, what people thought,
but the hurt ran deep. I felt ashamed.

A STRATEGY FOR EATING AN ORANGE

My mother would roll an orange under her foot before eating it.
She said it loosened the skin, made it much easier to peel.

I marvelled at this stroke of genius, watched my nanna do the same.
A kind of ritual, passed down from one generation to the next.

As a child I thought this was something everyone did - but not so
My best friend Sue had never heard of it. *You're weird* was her reaction.

And no, it's not in the bible, nor in Schott's compendium; it's more
a tradition, passed on orally. We never thought to question it.

And now I wouldn't hesitate each time I make a fruit salad
I simply take the Jaffa, place it under my foot and roll it round.

THE SWINGING SIXTIES

Argument over a maxi coat

My mum threw me that sideways glance,
said I looked absurd, that nobody wore
long coats nowadays.
Did I want to make an exhibition of myself?

I said everyone my age had them in London -
Trendy in Chelsea, uber-cool to wear one.
No one would turn and stare, unless with envy!

*What's more, you'll not walk with me
to chapel in it. I forbid you, do you hear?'*
She raced ahead, peeved, trying to disown me.

In London I aspired to be the epitome of cool,
a sex goddess, popping into *Bus Stop or Biba*
for a cheeky little Barbara Hulanicki number.

Back in my home town, not so.
Whispers, gossip, faces behind net curtains.
I rebelled, determined to shock prim neighbours
Look at me! I'm one of those weird hippy-chicks!

"I'm sure God doesn't care what I wear!" I said,
"Remember Mary Magdalene? She was a prostitute,
but Jesus loved her!"

MJB

It seemed a kindness,
not a thoughtless act
that caused her anger....
Just a fountain pen,
initials engraved on the side,
lent to a friend in class
when hers stopped working

My mother's expectations
were sometimes pitched too high...
Nine out of ten was good, praised,
But of course ten would be even better!
I studied the initials, M J B,
failing at first to see
another meaning beyond their link to me....

An 'M' for moderation - my mother,
between failure and perfection
no shades of grey for her;
for me a half-way compromise
Could I not fail just a little?

Then 'J' for Jessie, my aunt,
the embodiment of kindness;
her quiet smile afforded me
the possibility of being
purely and simply ME, warts and all

Finally a 'B', perhaps for books,
my escape to an alternative reality,
a place where my mind was free
to indulge my imagination,
to dream my childhood dream
of becoming a writer.

MY FATHER REKINDLES HIS YOUTH PLAYING 'BLAZE AWAY' ON OUR OLD PIANO

It marked the Sunday lunchtimes of my childhood,
him playing on our old piano, saved from a breaker's yard..

It gave him a buzz,
flashbacks to his Boys Brigade days:
club-swinging
      acrobatic displays   maze marching
         knot-tying   camping in rough terrain
the deafening cacophony of Tuesday night band practice
with bugles screaming blue murder.

He recalled those Sunday parades   bystanders tittering
as he barked commands from the front   *quick MARCH*
   left TURN   *halt*   *stand at........ EASE*
             Squad..... dis.....MISS!

He kept the foot-tapping rhythm going,
fingers skittering up and down the keyboard,
ignoring my mother's impassioned pleas:

Eddie, come to the table   right NOW!   dinner will spoil

My father ignored us all   transported back to
the glory days of his youth   football in the street
    barefoot cricket on the beach
screaming fans at Blundell Park Stadium.........until

the music book crashed from the stand, startling the cat,
bringing my mother rushing from the scullery,
wooden spoon in hand, wiping Yorkshire-pudding-battered
fingers on her apron, glowering at us over thick-rimmed specs.

Eddie, that's enough now. The beef's burning!
Time to sit up at table and say grace!

THE SECRET SERMONS

It began in Southampton   aged five.
The evangelist in me stirred an*d*   *(I wince ...)*
I preached my first sermon!
In the bemused congregation were my proud parents
plus our holiday hosts, the Louis family.

It was Sunday morning   yet no one was going to church.
Shock horror! That couldn't be right.
At home it was chapel three times on Sundays.

As a child I would sometimes go with my lay-preacher father
to far-flung Lincolnshire chapels on Sunday mornings.
The only attendees were usually farmers and their wives,
often just four or five people plus the odd cow or sheep
sticking their head through the door.
The organ required constant pumping,
something I loved to do when allowed.
I listened attentively to my father's sermons, though I didn't
really understand some of the words he used,
like *expedient* or *implicit* or *it behoves us.*

That day I arranged the chairs in the lounge,
brought extras in, along with a couple of hymnals.
Folk would have to share   but no matter   surely everyone
knew *All Things Bright and Beautiful* by heart, didn't they?

The somewhat unwilling worshippers filed in.
I took my place at the make-shift 'altar'
dressed in a white bed sheet serving as clerical gown.

I don't really remember the details   but allegedly
my sermon was twenty minutes long!
There was no stopping me once I got going.
I guess I must have trotted out words from all the
many sermons I'd been made to sit through back home.
No one dared titter or glance at their watch or venture a comment.
I think they probably tried not to laugh and thought me precocious.

Eight years later I gave a second sermon in my local chapel,
this time with less bravado.....
The theme was 'What the church has done for me.'
I recall extolling the virtues of Sunday School, Girls' Brigade,
of which I was a member - and Youth Club,
though the latter's attraction was certainly more about the
boys who hung out there and the possibility of snogging
one of them in the final Barn Dance when the lights went down!
Beyond that   what I preached is a bit of a blur.

MY DADDY, THE GENTLEMAN'S OUTFITTER

He always stacked the Trilby hats in rows,
dressed the faceless mannequins in worsted suits.
I'd perch like a sparrow on the counter top,
watching him unpack the stock.

Now and then his deep blue eyes threw me a winning smile.
My heart would leap, so proud that he was mine.
He worked long hours, lifting, lugging, sorting,
with *Workers Playtime* singing from the storeroom...
just like the Enid Blyton fathers in my favourite books.

A glamorous job, I thought, (too young to understand).
Yet later on, I saw how sweat seeped through his crisp white shirts
from hours of heaving, hoisting, humping stock.
As chain store goods began to steal his passing trade,
anxiety increased, frustration grew, he became withdrawn.

It stings my conscience now, the fact I never questioned
pain for gain; not seeing it was born of love.
His sacrifices meant that we could live guilt-free.
Today I cringe with guilt, because
what does that say about me?

A POSTCARD FROM SCARBOROUGH

Our old car scarcely made it
there and back, its engine
mostly cranked on hope
and fingers crossed.

Our destination Scarborough
in the 50s, about as far as
our faithful Austin 7 would go
without a mechanic on hand!

We always stayed at Mrs Gill's,
a modest boarding house
close to the sandy bay, where
pleasure boats winked sleepily

A cruise around the bay, then
fish and chips out of newspaper -
always the first thing on our list, though
thieving seagulls often spoiled the fun.

I think I was probably five years old
that time I got locked in the loo
at our B&B. Such utter panic!
It looms large in my memory even now...

We would ride the scenic railway, take the
bus to Peasholm Park, hire a rowing boat
or have a go on the putting green.
For me it was pure paradise.

The fun-packed week flew by, savouring
each day minute by joyful minute, sad when
our time was up and school called us home,
suitcases crammed with memories
to keep us going until next year.

FESTIVAL STRESS

Music festivals, oh what torture!
Sleepless nights, nerves jangling, stomach churning.

Whether piano or vocal pieces it was the same.
A compulsion to please parents and music teachers.

Show them how good you are!
You can beat Colin X and Yvonne Y into a cocked hat!

They were the ones convinced of my talent.
Me, I doubted their faith in me, tried to protest,
but couldn't say no.

Pressure to perform, like a barrel-organ monkey
Pressure to prove myself, make them proud.

Whose triumph or failure would it be anyway?
On reflection, no-one ever asked me how I felt.

THE BLACK HOLE OF CALCUTTA*

Twenty past four and already dark outside;
It's like the Black Hole of Calcutta in here.
My mother gives her verdict, shuffling quietly
past us in her carpet slippers that pad like a panther.
She stoops to fiddle with the lamp switch and
a dim halo of honey gold casts a shadow on the wall.

Calcutta, so distant, no context for us children,
though we had often asked the question.
She repeated the statement, more loudly now,
as though imagining that doing so would bring clarity,
rather like addressing a foreigner with no English...

We could usually anticipate which of her sayings was
about to tumble out from between her false teeth.
She seemed to have a store cupboard bursting full of them,
all strangely plucked from another time and space,
like odd plimsolls in an infants' cloakroom,
all higgledy-piggledy and no one caring a jot.

What's that about Calcutta?
Thirty years on and my daughter is curious.
I laugh out loud, realising I've entered a dark room
and immediately come out with the same thing.
Some family sayings just bridge the generation gap...
A history lesson on repeat.

The Black Hole of Calcutta was a dungeon in Fort William, Calcutta measuring 14 by 18 feet in which troops of Siraj-ud-Dallah, the Nawab of Bengal, held British prisoners of war on the night of 20 June 1756 as part of the siege of Fort William.

MY NANNA'S SAYINGS WERE PURE GOLD

'The day's not got up yet,' my nanna would say,
and I pictured clouds in a dormitory, lingering in bed,
mouths turned down at the corners, reluctant to
head downstairs in their marl- grey pyjamas.
The girl clouds were the worst, with their bed-head hair,
aghast at the very idea of rising and shining.

I wondered why they were not up on some days, yet
early risers in canary yellow suits on others?
I pictured a comely matron, black frock hugging
ample bosoms, stiff-starched white apron
straining across her stomach, chiding her brood
as they rushed downstairs to breakfast.

Were they punished for sleeping too long?
Did she whip them into shape? No doubt
those were days that brought a jungle roar of thunder,
lightning strikes on church steeples, stair-rod rain
pounding the earth like a toddler mid tantrum.

'Rain before seven, fine by eleven,' nanna would say. –
And I saw the rain cloud headmaster with stopwatch,
timing his pupils as they streamed from class to class.
She was usually right, though she never explained
how she knew. I guessed it was country superstition,
passed down from one generation to the next.

GRAMMAR SCHOOL MISCHIEF

We didn't give a damn about *Mother Courage* that day,
our young minds having better things to consider,
like catching Miss Rose kissing Mr Town
in the biology lab (school gossip!) –
though when we peered through the louvre blinds
we couldn't see anything at all!

That day we waited in the classroom for our
German teacher, Herr Langford.
Such an upright man of the cloth; ridiculously easy to deceive.
We were cruel Lolitas, feigning innocence,
mimicking him behind his back.

Hearing his Lutheran footsteps lumbering towards us,
we ducked down under the desks, kept schtum.
Hallelujah! No Brecht studies for us that day!
He stomped away and didn't report us - assumed
we had been excused class.

Yet now, guilt rises like bile in my throat,
whenever I think of those mean tricks we played.
I guess in truth he knew the score, felt humiliated.

INFANT SCHOOL PLAYTIME GONE WRONG

Another wet playtime,
a naive infant teacher with a new game.
a highly-strung six-year-old -
What could possibly go wrong?

Excited children, eager to evade the clutches of
Miss Wattam, the evil huntress.
Failure meant ending up in her giant cooking pot,
being eaten alive   *so she said.*
My six-year-old brain couldn't compute this.
What would my parents say? How would they react?

The classroom was small, Victorian, high windows.
Already the bully boys were shoving, elbowing..
I squeezed my tiny frame between the cupboard
and the fireplace, curled up like a hedgehog in a ball.
Too late! She'd spotted me, pounced on her prey,
her strong arms pulling me protesting from my hidey-hole.

No compassion. I was penned in with the others
behind her huge desk.
Sidney Cotton poked me in the ribs and laughed out loud.
'Don't be so daft. It's just a game,' he said.
'Miss, Miss, she thinks it's real.'

Miss Wattam suddenly realised she had
a traumatised child on her hands.
She sat me on her lap, stroked my hair.

'It's just a game. Don't be frightened.
I'm not really going to eat you.'

Oh the sheer relief! I recall it so vividly now.
I suddenly felt embarrassed by my stupidity.
Yet looking back I wonder who was the stupid one?
Me, or her?
I certainly never trusted her again.

COAL DELIVERIES CAUSE PROBLEMS FOR OUR CAT

Coal deliveries were a noisy affair. The coal lorry came laden high with enormous coal sacks.
It would drive up our eight-foot*, park up by the old Anderson shelter* and the delivery men would then noisily tip the sacks into the big bunker in the back yard. It sounded like thunder.
As a child it startled me. I disliked it intensely and would run off to my bedroom, holding my ears. Our cat, Corky, was alarmed when the delivery men came and as a young cat she would jump inside the piano, only to emerge once they had departed. This went on for several years until on one occasion, having grown into a fully mature cat, she jumped inside but was unable to clamber out again! We didn't notice at first, then became aware of an urgent scraping noise coming from the living room. We traced the source of the sound to the old piano and worked out that Corky was unable to jump out this time. In order to release her we needed to remove the piano's front panel. It goes without saying that Corky learned her lesson and from then on never again tried to hide there. Instead she faced the coal men head on, hissing and growling.

*eight-foot, local dialect for a passageway between buildings approximately eight feet wide.
*Anderson shelter, a World War 11 air-raid shelter

MY MOTHER FEIGNS KNOWLEDGE OF FRENCH

In the early 50's Mum was shopping at Penistone's local grocery - a time when post-war rationing was still in place. Shelves were stocked with family necessities: packets and tins arranged like fledglings teetering on the brink, bright-eyed with hope. Her list had none of today's luxuries – just basic foods like eggs, flour, milk, margarine, leaf tea, cheese, bovril.
We ate just to stay alive. Mum proudly followed my school work. With nanny a war widow her options had been few, but she was keen to learn some basic French vocabulary with me.

A French couple were shopping that day, but with little success. They had no English at all, but my Mum recognised the words they were saying and mustered up the courage to chip in and help by saying she believed it was flour and eggs that they wanted, quickly pointing out these items on the shelves. The assistant was delighted and the couple nodded their gratitude. 'Oh Madam, you've just saved my life,' said the girl, ' thank goodness you can speak fluent French!' My Mum simply smiled, kept the truth to herself, but inwardly she felt ten feet tall.

SNOWDROP SECRETS

Seeing the first snowdrops reminds me of a secret my aunt and I once shared. It was a moment of intimacy that bound us together, a secret unknown to the rest of the family. Only decades later was it mentioned again, this time by a healer, from whom I sought comfort after the trauma of 1998. Her words caused the hairs on the back of my neck to stand up and chills to run down my spine. How could she possibly know about that event? It seemed impossible to me. Did this clairvoyant possess supernatural powers? During our chat she had tuned in to an item of my aunt's jewellery and had gone on to describe her character exactly. It was too uncanny for words and threw me off balance. I was sceptical that this really could be my Aunt Jessie, so she attempted to win me over: '*You've shared a secret, just the two of you, something to do with snowdrops perhaps?*' It brought a host of suppressed childhood memories flooding right back, one of which was a Sunday school song about snowdrops pushing through the hard soil, defying the cold, reaching the light and lovingly embracing one another. The music was so sad and I sobbed every time we sang it! I think it was the harsh words of the song that depressed me so much: *Dead, said the frost, buried and lost, every one;* so much so that I begged my aunt not to make us sing the song at the anniversary celebrations. She sympathised but explained she couldn't make an exception for me, her niece. But to help me through she devised an effective strategy. We never told anyone! So when the healer brought it up I was completely thrown. However, my head was so full of all the wonderful things my dear aunt and I had done together that I instantly knew she had to be telling the truth.

SUMMER ON CLEETHORPES BEACH

A sestina

When rose-pink streaks the sky at break of day
the backdrop of my childhood summons me
to saunter down the slipway at high tide
and watch the breakers crashing on the shore,
recalling carefree days when life was slow;
we children roamed at will, content and free.

The simple things in life were mostly free
of charge, We'd linger on the beach each day,
where patient donkeys trotted, gentle, slow,
their threepenny rides a summer treat for me.
On donkey-back we'd trot along the shore
but watch out for the turning of the tide.

So dangerous, we knew, that trickster tide,
remembered that thick pea soup fog, the free
-dom snatched away from riders on the shore;
an unexpected tragedy that day.
Grief swept throughout the town, it haunted me;
the children's gruesome deaths, untimely, slow.

Most days we'd play for hours, watch as the slow
sun sank on red horizon and the tide
drew back into the cold North Sea.... for me
and best friend time to leave, hair streaming free,
run home for family tea at close of day,
relate our bold adventures on the shore.

The locals took brisk walks along the shore,
including pensioners, whose pace was slow -
there was no need for haste, they had all day
to stroll and sit, observe the rising tide,
or catch a show ... the pier ones often free;
to see them holding hands delighted me.

Soul sister Judith used to call for me;
together we would chase down to the shore,
build mud pies, sandcastles, sometimes we'd free
-load at the shrimp stall, savouring the slow
drip of saliva down our chins...... a tide
of joyful memories floods my mind today.

The hours stretched out for her and me, time slow
on that wild shore eroded by the tide.
We wandered free, savoured each passing day.

AUNT JESSIE'S DEVON VIOLETS PERFUME

My Aunt Jessie was kindness personified.
I cherished her empty 'Devon violets' scent bottles:
lavender butterfly hearts strewn across ample bosoms,
a tsunami of petals holding back the reprimands
that never could get past the tip of her tongue.
They bathed my bones in fragrant lullabies,
bandaged grazed knees, hummed healing spells
over sick beds of measles and mumps.
Each time she dabbed perfume behind her ears
the dust and clay of past and future ebbed and flowed;
I trusted in the moment, happy in my skin.

SPURN POINT LIGHTHOUSE

Bleak spur of ashen land
eroded constantly by
cruel storm's thrust

Between timed flashes
breath held in awe, the blinding
beam splitting the stars

There for a wave-surge
then gone, the tidal backwash
scourging the Point

A GRIM RECOLLECTION

*Response to lines from T.S Eliot's poem 'The Love Song of
J Alfred Prufrock'*

*'I shall wear white flannel trousers, and walk upon the beach,
I have heard the mermaids singing each to each'*

We drift like ghosts in mist along the creek,
where no one lingers on the mudflats
to delve into memory's deep pools.

Too well the locals know the fate
of innocents who walk the 'coffin track'
across to Hale Fort;
trouser legs rolled high,
eager to beat the tide,
to reach a World War fortress,
guardian of the Humber estuary.

'The tide, beware the turning of the tide,'
the mermaids call from siren sanctuaries,
their fin-tails hidden by comely bodies;
nemesis of many a hapless walker.

And look, already the first trickles
snake their path along the creek-bed,
sly serpents sliding over shingle,
the current forking where boulders
block an onward path...
More quickly now, a rushing race,
filling the creek, false-footing the unwary.
Look, see how easily they could drown!

Let us hurry back to the beach, remember
that day when gathering sea mist morphed to fog,
engulfing novice riders in pure panic.
Their cries of desperation haunt my dreams.
They steered the ponies round towards the shore,
yet wrongly guessed direction, allowing
the tide to gush in around them from behind.

Such tragedy must not happen ever again!
Let us grab the bridles,
swing the gentle creatures round,
blow a ghost-wind at their backs,
think them safely ashore...
No matter the torn trousers around our knees;
folk like us have no need of human apparel.

A CHILD'S RECURRING NIGHTMARE AFTER A DROWNING

Stand still! Look how the sea is drawn to you.
Dark magnetism pulls you closer in,
and you would wade in deep in socks and shoes,
replay once more that haunting childhood scene –
that drowning man. *Act now, girl, pull him out!*
The tide turns, sweeps him back, he can't push on
Your mother sleeps, the coastguard's on a shout,
the lifeguard clocked off early.... You're the one!

I was a child, afraid, too mute to scream
though black clouds loomed and storms were imminent
Was this reality, or just a dream?
A ten year old the only saviour sent?

Desist! There's nothing more that could be done -
Forgiveness is not needed   life moves on.

EYE OF A COASTAL STORM

Surge of anger   birthed from torn sky's womb
ripping   rending apart the senses
sucking strength from fragile bones

sand scree shifting   duped by smokescreens
raptors skimming a drowning wasteland
waves warping the weft of transient time

the mind buffeted   broken like a young stallion
vision impaired
          fading scrawl   signposts blurring
blank screen behind eyelids

feet thrusting through mire of mud in
torrential downpour   patience exhausted
        bulging eye of the storm
Big Brother biding his time   planning the kill.

AN UNDESIRABLE STUDENT JOB AT BIRD'S EYE

Inspired by A E Housman's 'Yonder See The Morning'

Thank God that daylight ends this hell,
this night-shift in a factory hall
with rogue peas shimmying by en masse
I had to grab as they danced past,
with vile black cockroaches as well.

Dark hours on shift with trance-like gaze;
and yet good reason for my toil –
each week a decent wage for me
brought trips to France and Germany ...
Dark memories though time won't erase!

THE STONES OF LINCOLN CATHEDRAL

Built straight onto rock, these stone walls have spoken to me from early childhood on. They were my escape, the saviour of my youth. Their towering spires drew my childlike gaze upwards to the wide skies above, to boundless possibilities; freedom for body and soul, desired but untasted. This glorious edifice still stands firm, surviving the toughest tests of time. What history these stones have seen. What stories they can tell. I walk the cobblestones and feel the memories seeping through, find messages in the limestone... The Mayflower graffiti, carved into stone on an inner pillar, well hidden from view; the legendary Lincoln Imp, perched cross-legged high up in the dome; sent to carry out the Devil's dirty work, wreaking havoc until an angry angel stepped in, turned him to stone. Of all the great cathedrals in this land, whether domed, towered, or spired, this is the one that fills me most with wonder, takes my breath away. I could sit here in the shadow of its magnificence, listen to the stones humming with myth and magic, watch the world go by and feel the ghostly stomp of feet marching over cobblestones, relic of a Roman city's glorious past. If you tune in, the stones will speak to you, imparting their ancient wisdom.

BENEATH THE COVERS WITH RADIO LUXEMBOURG AND OTHER COOL DUDE STUFF

When my grandfather died in my teens I was gifted a battery operated transistor radio. They were all the rage back then. This meant I could sneak off to bed with radio and torch and under the bedcovers I could listen to the Top Thirty countdown on Sunday nights. What a delicious secret! I could keep up with the latest pop music, record sales and everything a 'hip' teenager needed to know. The torch under the sheets was key, removing the necessity to switch on the bedroom light, thus alerting my parents to this illegal activity. Due to the station's freedom to advertise commercially, (not allowed on the BBC,) Radio Luxembourg ran many memorable adverting campaigns, whose details will be easily recalled by ardent listeners of the time. For me the standout one was from Horace Batchelor, who had a patented method for winning big on the pools. Listeners simply had to write to him free at '*Department 1, Keynsham, that's K-E-Y-N-S-H-A-M* (there were no postcodes back then!) I have cherished memories of secret nights, cosy under the sheets (no duvets, just sheets, blankets and quilts back then.) Some famous names of the era were Barry Adill, Kid Jensen, Pete Murray and Kenny Everett. Being an avid fan meant you could listen in to real Rock n' Roll, making you a 'hip cat', most certainly not 'square' (a conformist to social mores.) If you wore the trendy black gear of the times you were probably a beatnik. Oh how little it took in those days to get our hearts pounding, as we drooled over the local dreamboat (a fit male) or blushed at being called a 'doll' with a 'classy chassis'.We thought we were the bees knees in our hooped dresses with their paper nylon underskirts, worn over roll-ons with suspenders and nylon stockings with seams up the back.The place to get frisky with your date was in the back row at the flicks (cinema) or in an old banger where you could play 'back seat bingo.' Boys or girls who were a bit too keen to 'get jiggy' with multiple partners were labelled 'fast', but of courses there was no contraceptive pill back then, so girls thought twice re indulging in pre-marital sex. It was an era of simple day-dreaming, uncomplicated by the social media of today. I am so relieved that I was born post-war when life was much more straightforward, less of a maze. Life's pleasures were simple and cost little by comparison.

GETTING READY FOR THE FRESHERS' DISCO

I slick a layer of scarlet gloss
over virgin-plump lips, paint rag-doll pink
on pale cheeks, emulating my flatmates.

But their come-to-bed looks are not for me.
Why am I even trying to copy them?
I swig vodka straight from the bottle   then wince.

My flatmates are competing for mirror space,
creating Lolita faces with consummate skill.
Cheap tarts, my mother would say.

Methodist guilt rises in the pit of my stomach,
laced with a frisson of excitement -
If only my mother could see me now!

Oh yes, she would totally disapprove!
I glance at my reflection in the mirror and ponder
whether the new look is actually *me?*

I'm not so sure. After eighteen years at home
under the thumb, this is the freedom I have craved for so long ...
But now I have it, I'm uncertain what to do with it.

HOMESICK FOR FRAU MECKES' KITCHEN

Memories of my year teaching in Germany

How often I've thought about
that heady aroma of coffee beans,
that buzz in the grinder, a swarm of trapped bees,
that Rosenthal coffee pot teetering on the shelf;
the previous night's pile of *Salzkartoffeln* *
calling to my grumbling belly from the counter top.
I always wondered if anyone would miss a few?

And my landlady, Frau Meckes, in her black widow's weeds,
bun pulled tight to her crown, walking in with her
don't-you-dare-mess-with-me face, hitching up
her wrinkled Pippi Langstrumpf stockings.

And then, another filmic moment -
mist drifting in from the Rhine on an October day...
I pause to reflect how complex language is,
how strange that in German *Mist* means rubbish!
I recall my English pupils falling off their chairs
when I said, *it's misty* today....
(but they never forgot the word again!)

Today I picture myself in that kitchen,
sampling a few of those cold potatoes,
my mouth watering at the smell of left-over sausage;
the kitchen clock ticking noisily, and on the hour
the cuckoo bursting forth, showing off.

I could die for a slice of *Schwarzwälderkirschtorte,* *
just like I used to order in Karstadt café.
Someone, please transport me back there, let me
relive the moment when that dishy young waiter
first set down the plate oozing with whipped cream.

My eyes well up with tears, recalling that year I
came of age, 1966....and suddenly I'm overcome
by an acute dose of *Heimweh.*

*Salzkartoffeln – salted boiled potatoes.   * Schwarwälderkirschtorte – Black Forest gâteau.*

VILLANELLE FOR THE FIRST MEN ON THE MOON

Those first three men who landed on the moon
Were surely hoping they would all survive
Their families prayed they'd fly home safely soon.

They showed great calm and strength, a massive boon
Though privately they all feared for their lives
Those first three men who landed on the moon.

They listened to the radio's poignant tunes
Reminding them of children, home and wives
Their families hoped they'd fly home very soon.

Sometimes to lift their mood they'd act the goon
With playful space-manoeuvres, swerves and dives,
Those first three men who landed on the moon.

They gathered moon rocks lunar winds had strewn
Ate food from tubes, no scope for forks or knives
Their families hoped they'd fly home very soon.

Job done they launched their craft into the gloom
Like honey bees that buzzed back to the hive.
Their families glad they'd flown back very soon....
Those first three men who landed on the moon.

BRAMBLING

Inspired by the poetry of Ruth Stone

All my life I've been brambling;
plopping plump promises into my mouth,
twirling the bitter sweetness around my tongue,
eyes screwed up when the sourness kicked in.
As teenagers we would bike round 'Ginger's,'
its hedgerows boasting a bumper crop,
bushier than Grandpa's eyebrows.
Once home I'd bake bramble pies for tea.
I recall one Sunday evening my son's bombshell -
cookery next day   blackberry pie   did we have any?
A quick foray down the local lanes thankfully yielded
a 'plentiful sufficiency,'as my dad used to say.
But those barbs! I have suffered their curse
more often than I care to recall. Thorns ripping flesh.
My first love tricked me with vain promises -
'Blackberry pie tomorrow   soon   next week...'
More fool me, blanking out the obvious.
My first marriage hurled me into razor-sharp thickets
so dense that emerging proved almost impossible.
Inch by inch I crawled out backwards before I drowned...
But it takes way more than that to keep a Lincolnshire lass
from brambling!

PART TWO: INTERMEZZO:

The downside of growing up with high-pitched parental and community expectations

MISFIT

Feeling different

Standing on the edge of the circle
I watched
           from a modest distance.

Unlike theirs, my shirt was made of calico,
(yet equally fit for purpose, I imagined)

I was unacknowledged   overlooked.

Perhaps the shirt had a missing button,
an omission that excluded me,
painted a bindi on my forehead
only visible to them?

But how could I remedy this?
I had no buttons that fitted the holes!

Their shuffling feet trampled my breathing,
mud-heavy voices spoke in a language
unfamiliar to me.

Had I betrayed myself,
a wolf in sheep's clothing?
They turned to stare with cold contempt,
yet simply found
a sartorially confused stranger....

They mouthed spiteful words, but I could lipread!

Now was the moment to confront,
to protest my allegiance to their tribe...
Yet instead

I turned

I fled

My buttons did not fit their shirts;
they never would!
I was forever *persona non grata.*

FLAMINGO GIRL

I'm watching her dancing, remembering
what it was like to be skinny and pretty
with legs that reached to heaven   and
the whole world at my feet...

A flamingo on stilts   graceful   elegant
pirouetting across the stage of life
back in those halcyon days   now shrouded in mist.
Whatever happened to the years in between?

Pink ballet shoes went off to a charity shop,
pink tutu passed down to a young pretender,
silver medals stowed away in shabby cardboard boxes...

Nowadays I dance in my dreams   happy in my skin.

DILEMMA

I'm standing on the sideline,
watching grief unfolding,
flapping on the breeze like
Nanna's patched bedsheets,
pastel pink flamingos
stiff-winged   feet mired in mud.

I note my hesitance   my confusion,
wondering if silence is better
than intimate betrayal?

But silence, like Chinese whispers,
might destroy what remains of us;

never again to stroll down memory lane
giddy with passion   arms entwined
through Notting Hill;
twenty-somethings on Saturday afternoons,
innocent lovers in bohemia.

My gut feeling says anonymity, yes
way to go, my friend –

that youthful *liaison*
was simply

          too

              dangereuse

GRIEF IS A DEAD RAVEN

I am immodestly naked
in their playground;
a raven
     fallen
        from a yew tree
half-wrapped in a joyless hello.

A plump boy is lighting matches,
intent on igniting me,
     zapping my doomed carcass.
His fists pummel me,
repulsing the snatching claws
of his devil-spawned classmates
        crowding in for the kill.

And from the staff room window
Miss Jackson is yelling profanities,
deep   dark   disturbing

They splash up from the vampire-black
tarmac yard,

       the one
         where

my unborn grandchildren will never ever play!

A LOVE-HATE RELATIONSHIP WITH MY DARK UNDER-EYE CIRCLES

They haunted me from an early age, these
ink stains smeared across delicate ivory skin,
tainting the dewy blossom of my youth.

Even as a baby they were there, as though someone
had used indelible ink to draw a cartoon feature
above the cheekbones, christening me ugly.

My mother had them too; I cursed her bones
for that, condemning me to a life of camouflage,
set apart from the pageant queens of pushy mums,

never in their league, always the last to be chosen.
Heavy under the eyes, was what they said, or
You look tired   have you been crying?

Mirrors? Oh I've always hated them,
could not look myself in the eye, turned away
sulking, hiding behind the comfort of a curtain fringe.

That's not me, not the real me. I was deluded.
To go unnoticed I wore a ghost shroud in public,
a walking apology for my lack of self-belief.

I'm at fever pitch when a new ad runs on TV
for a miracle concealer, *hides dark circles like magic!*
And I rush out, a nude-faced convert in sunglasses

to that holy of holies, the John Lewis cosmetics counter,
worshipping like an acolyte at the altar of Aphrodite,
hope muting the nagging voice in my head that says

It probably won't work! And yes, I know it's just hype.
But recently I had a big aha moment, when someone
told me I had 'come-to-bed' eyes and I whooped for joy.

MIND OVER MATTER

Living with rheumatoid arthritis at its worst

I *could* describe to you my slow
morning routine in painful detail;
yet I choose to share the harsh reality
with only a privileged few.

The alarm rings at seven.
Two hours to get the stiff limbs moving,
almost crawling at first, holding on to
furniture, clinging limpet-like
to the bannister in sideways snail-crawl.
I pop the pills that keep me going,
swilling them down with sparkling water
laced with honey and apple cider vinegar.

Dressing is slow.
Almost like target practice,
matching up trouser leg and foot,
creakily bending to slot feet into socks.
It takes me a good half hour.

Concealer to disguise my panda eyes,
a generous sweep of blusher   peach pink works best;
then scarlet Marilyn Monroe lips in a Cupid's bow
to disguise the fibs I have to tell.

"Looking good today, such a healthy glow"
my friends may exclaim..
I don't contradict, simply smile.
They have no idea of the cunning strategy
required to make palatable
my appearance in public today.
Pride prevents me from divulging the detail.
I have mastered the art of deception
and intend to keep it that way.
It's simply a case of mind over matter,

BECAUSE I'M WORTH IT!

Sometimes the creep of time weighs heavy on the mind.
Memory is a cruel trickster, trifling with the brain...

Lost youth brings many a regret; that face in the mirror
staring rudely back at me like an old hag.... *who is SHE?*

the sudden recognition, far too real,
too close for comfort, so I look away.

Could self-belief be the antidote...
Learning to be happy in one's own skin?

We might need to lie down on the therapist's couch.....
let the hypnotist cure us of our phobias,

wriggle free of that cruel imposter syndrome -
Join a dance class, take an art course,

Start writing that novel! (There's a book in all of us, they say.)
Whatever it takes to turn the page and start afresh,

Just do it now...because at the end of the day
we are all worth it!

CHARISMA IN THE THIRD AGE

This face is yesterday's rose...deliciously crumpled,
mapping out ancient well-trodden pathways,
shedding fragrant petals to reveal an inner luminescence,
a scent of musk now permeating fading beauty.

Flashbacks dart across the mind's eye like butterflies:
ritual bathing at the healing well, drinking chalice water,
dancing on dewdrop toes beneath rippling willows,
weaving leafy garlands in the dark silence of druids' caves.

Voluptuousness trickles from a love spoon,
once youthful skin hauntingly etched by the sands of time,
still radiating that irresistible lure of autumnal charm,
the face of an English Rose, reborn in its third age.

ALLOW ME TO BE ME

Do not paint my portrait,
for I have a changing face
that alters with age.

Do not declaim me in verse,
for I am a fledgling poet
undefined by genre.

Do not photograph me,
for I am a free spirit
not confined to time and space.

Do not dance my dance,
for I am a swirling ribbon
unrestricted by routine.

Do not sing my song,
for I may have a new lament
not yet composed.

Do not aspire to know me,
for I grow in wisdom and change....
Allow me to be **ME**!

PART THREE: FUGUE

Flashbacks in present time to influences from the decades in between, aligned with the colours and sounds of life's rich musical score

Each poem here has a suggestion of a colour and piece of music to accompany it.

WALKING BETWEEN THE ANCIENT WELLS – A WALKING MEDITATION IN 13 STAGES

Colour:Rainbow hues / Music: *Bach, Toccata and Fugue*

1)

The country lane snakes ahead, jewelled with hoar-frost tracery;
turning my thoughts to local tales of myth and magic;

frayed threads silver the silent track ahead,
hemming together meadows, farms and coppices.

I step out into the shock of frozen air, lungs gasping from the slap,
embracing the crackle of snow-crisped gravel underfoot.

A lone robin brushes past my hood, inviting companionship,
his russet underbelly a token of winter's fireside embers.

Wayside fences sulk beneath the heft of drifting snow,
slats spilling out onto the lane, snagging unwary feet.

Morning is still only half-awake, building up to future glory,
her bed-head lethargy burns deep into my consciousness.

2)

The familiar patchwork of fields bordering the road is concealed,
donkey-brown furrows in hiding, shivering beneath snow shrouds.

I pause, listen to the burbling of the eager brook, flooded by recent rain,
hurtling over boulders, under bridges, eager to make a land grab.

No birdsong audible today. Flora and fauna are in hibernation;
cattle in winter quarters stamp impatient hooves, trample soiled bedding,

Stallions long to feel again the spent summer's warmth on their backs,
tossing unkempt manes, plotting an escape from winter confinement.

I sense their repression, the need to fly their spirits high like a child's kite.
I too sense that urgency, the need to push on, one step at a time.

3)

As I approach the bend my favourite oak tree
leans in conversationally for a winter hug.

I cherish our long friendship;
we have no need of words
I am his, he is mine

A sturdy trunk with
multiple offshoots swathed in
trailing ivy fronds

Ageing boughs reach upwards,
pushing towards the waning light
with strong sense of purpose

As I run my hands
across the rough, tough gnarled bark
I sense contentment.

My friend has stood here
for many a year and will
be here when I'm gone

Generations will
pass him by, yet sadly not
love him as I do.

4)

Above me now a Payne's grey pall descends, shafts of light piercing
through gathering cloud, reminiscent of paintings by Friedrich or Munch....

That mastery of shock, a daubing of oils here, a bold impasto there,
a confrontation of past and present, sublimating the blank canvas.

As storm clouds muster like sky-troopers, masking the steeple
weathercock,
a murder of startled crows, wings spread wide, scythes past my head.

Checking my backpack for stout waterproof, berry-bright like a sunset sky,
I recall the country shepherd's oft quoted adage.... *red sky in the
morning......*

I heed the warning, seek shelter in a nearby barn.

5) *With a nod to Edward Thomas' March 3rd*

As I shelter, filmic memories swirl in my head,
returning me to milder autumn days, when
fields stood harvest-ready and the moon leaned in low
over the farm gate, in awe of the season's bounty.

Those were halcyon days
for harvesting; for the
daylight hours were dry and fair
as Indian summer.

We walked the stubble fields
from Aurora's unveiling
of stippled skies
to Morpheus' nightshade.

Such days of plenitude,
the russet hours full-tamed;
our thought flow morphed to poetry.

6)

And then my thoughts slip back to childhood summers,
to emerald meadows, romancing the lure of Constable's idylls:

calves almost fully grown, recumbent in lush pastures of
vetch and clover, chewing the cud of monotony,
instinct their master, unburdened by human preoccupations.

We would saunter arm in arm down Hardy's Lane, stopping at the farm
to tease Billy the bull with his gleaming coat and menacing eyes,
venturing to tickle his back with braids of goose grass, making him bellow..

Along the hedgerows drunken bees dozed in campion throats,
a light breeze tickled the foliage, ruffled the surface of the stream.
As the blue hour extended its fingertips, pushing back the night,
we headed back home to the warmth of our mothers' outstretched arms.

7)

As I perch on a bale of hay, a summer memory
demands to be revisited; tears prickle my eyes:

The day I gave birth to my first-born
the hares were leaping on Potter Hill.
Hazy sun, pale as peach bloom, spread naked wings
to start its ascent to glory.

Along the lanes cow-parsley hummed its
simple plainsong, curtseyed with sage smile.
That raw innocence of first light; a sacred promise
on an unknown brink.

It was as though the whole world hummed,
as he wriggled in my tightening womb and
sweat dripped from my anxious brow.
I tasted the future - the raw, naked bones of it.

By evening, as the spent sun dropped low and
twilight's salve slipped down my fevered cheeks,
my new-born simpered, contented in his cot
and Morpheus' fingers closed drooping eyelids.

8)

And earlier in the year   spring   strutting her peacock pomp,
surprising us with an early fashion show,
lifting the caul from sleepy eyes, calling to us,
'Carpe Diem, while youth's dew still blesses your bones'.

Returning swallows fussing over familial habitats,
last year's nests still intact under drooping eaves.
Blossoms of cherry, apple and plum, a heady aroma
filling the nostrils, assuring us of future plenty in granary and barn.

The images twist and tumble, like beads in a kaleidoscope:
the bluster of March gales -
the elegance of an Easter daffodil ballet -
the sweet tang of April raindrops on the lips -
the Maypole hoisted on the village green.....

How intricate the finer details in my mind's eye as the storm rips through.

9)

Yet behind the beauty of each rural scene
lies a truth that is harder to swallow.
At first glance all seems perfect...

Dappled early morning light,
clear dew drops reflecting grey sky,
lambs with pink tongues
tussling for first pull of lush stems,
last supper imminent.

Cygnets strutting like mannequins
down dusty tracks towards village ponds.
Rumbling of distant thunder,
damp ditches steaming.

Overhead rowdy crows trumpeting
loud morning reveilles,
rudely stirring woodland creatures
from winter sleep.

Early hunter-gatherers
chancing upon swathes of
star-petalled lesser celandine
nestling in ancient clearings.
And up above the scheming cuckoo
stealing nesting rights from pipits and warblers...

And so the scene replays; *perpetuum mobile...*

Yet this is no pastoral idyll...
Nature quakes, as ruddy cheeked farmhands
leap into tractor cabs, work-weary engines
sputter into action, crop-spray ready....

Then gagged fields and hedgerows
suffer in silence the indignity of toxic rape.

10)

Moving on I hear it already from half a mile away,
that urgent crescendo of sound, a jungle roar,
feel the rush of trembling air like dragon's breath.

The electric monsters come flying down the tracks
carrying their human cargo ... York- or Durham-
Newcastle- or Edinburgh-bound.

Ten - always ten - coaches with puppet heads
at the windows, whizzing past at break-neck speed.
Impossible to catch what they are doing:
paring an apple, unpacking a sandwich,
reading a spell-binding thriller, writing a memo,
chatting on mobile phones or typing on laptops.

Contemporary life condensed into minute detail,
in limbo land as the puppets are catapulted from
A to B, lethargy or frustration a compass of mood.

The monsters roar past and the parrot's cage is raised.
Impatient motorists rev up and accelerate, irritated by
protracted delay, sometimes four or five trains fly past. .

11)

Light drizzle now morphs to sleet.

A red-ringed lollipop etched with an ink-black '30'
greets me with candied smile as I enter the village.

A hotchpotch of sleepy farmsteads, wide-eyed bungalows
and restored cottages from the Civil War era rub shoulders here.

Parked cars on drives have donned winter overcoats, windows
obscured. Who knows what tittle-tattle passes behind shutters!

I zip my coat up to the neck, pull down my hat over frizzy curls,
clapping my mittened hands together to restore circulation.

For less hardy folk today is a day for hearthside comforts,
for banking up the coal fire, toasting crumpets, indulging in armchair
travel.

But needs must. My 10,000 steps must be accomplished before I hang
my dripping coat on the hook and park my sodden boots in the porch.

12)

I recall harsher winters than this as a young child
growing up in Lincolnshire...

It was bone-chillingly cold.
Lakes and streams frozen solid,
icicles hanging from gutters and eaves
like the sword of Damocles.
Spider's webs, starched like
city-slickers' collars, clinging rigidly
to fences and hedgerows.
Snow drifts piled high
as the driving blizzard took hold.
Buildings glared like mausoleums...
No transport, no public services,
No end in sight for that bitter Winter!
Animals and humans chose hibernation.

Only a lone skater, clad in an Eskimo skin,
cut through the thick ice on the local pond,
skate blades flashing in the moonlight.

13)

At last I reach my journey's end,
weary and foot-sore,
feet blistered,
fingers blue inside mittens.

My village sign comes into view;
the church tower silhouetted
against a gunmetal sky.
I summon up a final burst of energy,
cross over by the vicarage ....
and I am home.

My little cat is waiting in the porch.
She rushes to me, tail held high,
rubbing against my legs, chirruping,
her greeting clearly fired by feline hope......
Indeed, there will be dainty treats for us both tonight!

A PRECIOUS GIFT

A set of amber jewellery brought back for me
by my husband from his time working in Tajikistan

Colour: Amber / Music: *Beethoven's Moonlight Sonata*

Mellifluous beauty
nectar of the gods
minute resin crystals
less dense than stone
yet too dense to float
heterogeneous in composition
may contain small insects
glimmering like midday sunshine
a lamp to light the way.
My amber ring
my heart stone
a love token
brought back
by my husband
from Tajikistan
adorning my ring finger
set in a silver scroll
always with me,
guardian of what was
soothsayer for what may be
honey for life's future burns
key to unlock memories
never to be erased
life's ebb and flow
glinting gold
winking in
fractal moonlight
a forever friend -
eternal love

Colour: Blue/ Music: *Rachmaninoff, Variations on a theme by Paganini, opus 43, variation 18*

The Blue Hour

I remember him best of all in Norfolk,
sauntering through evening meadows,
the blue hour weaving its special charm.

We floated on air   hovered above limpid streams
each in-breath held   waiting
each of us part of a collective rhythm,
exhaling softly   lungs squeezed like a concertina.

Spectators in nature   speaking in whispers
respectful   this territory theirs not ours.

This was a world where vulnerability cowered;
the fleet of foot, wily of wing   here   then gone.
Water voles in velvet suits, puppet fox with invisible
strings   playful   crouching low   then scenting danger
        slinking back to the leash.

A swoop of ghost-owl   hunter with razor-sharp beak
wings scything the dusk   then a curdling cry
a field mouse trapped in the pincer grip of talons;
life inextricably linked to death.

A privileged viewing   yet looking back
I sometimes wonder if it was real   or was it simply a dream
conjured up with him at the heart of it...
            where he always was?

Colour: Blood Red/ Music: *Fields of Gold, Eva Cassidy*

Last hour at a hospice bedside

Above the drone of constant chatter
the fading strains of hope's last stand -
Rachmaninoff on a rogue radio.
The aroma of freshly popped toast,
buttered with grief, clings like smog.
Everywhere relentless trivia intrude,
as invisible blood drips from my wounds,
pooling into a lake of deep crimson, like the hips
on the winter rose bush beyond the hospice window.

Glioblastoma devours his brain -
grade four, no treatment, bad prognosis...
'Take him home to die, enjoy
what time is left,'advises the specialist.
His words trip far too lightly off his feral tongue,
as though he is dictating a memo, dispassionate.
I struggle to find a morsel of forgiveness.

Gritting my teeth, I steel myself
for the grim hours ahead, maybe just minutes?
He is drifting away from me second by second.
One last heart-stopping time I stoop
and bathe his withered lips with my tears,
then, all too soon the last   breath   comes,
gently, like a dove settling on an olive branch.

Unexpectedly I feel a sudden sense of relief.

Colour: Green/ Music: *Ralph Vaughan Williams, The Lark Ascending, Hilary Hahn violin*

Hilltop Panorama

Each hilltop with its panorama,
360 degrees of lush indulgence
for the eyes, a pointillist patchwork
crowned with verdant foliage,
tall grasses, streams awash with
impressionist watercolour reflections;
the zenith of Nature's pure intent.

Truth greens here, overcomes envy.
At its centre the heart journeys
towards peace, connects the gifts
of knowledge and speech, harnessing
the chakra powers of gold and mid blue.
Rainbows arc the sky in Cupid's love bows,
initiate a paradigm shift in green.

Colour: Pale Yellow/ Music: *Creedence Clearwater Revival, Bad Moon Rising*

Halloween

Muffled strike of weary clocks as
evil prowls the midnight hour,
storms gather in a blotting paper sky
heavy with ink of darkest fantasy..

She walks the wilderness of rain-drenched streets,
facades of faded villas lurk like ghosts,
still draped in swags from former glory days.

Danger crouches like a thief in alleyways,
on Gallows Hill a ghostly scaffold looms,
protruding through the rough-sewn cloth of night.
Deep in the graveyard's pit damp bones
shudder in their tattered shrouds.

Last bus long gone, taxis on strike tonight.

She scurries home, her Jimmy Choos
click-clacking rhythmically on hollow stones,
determination in her stride.

'Beware the evil moon tonight!'
that's what the local folk had said.
She jumps at every sudden sound:
fighting cats on slippery roofs
drink cans whistling past her feet.

Gripping keys and iPhone, she tells herself
it's stupid talk, just local superstition
but   scurrying home   her thumb hovers on 9......
just in case...

Colour: Purple/ Music: *Storms in Africa, Enya*

October Wasteland

Bare stalls decay
         destroyed by elemental siege
in fields where harvest kings
         once wore their glittering crowns.

A boy plucks withered bounty from the hedgerow
         purple lips inked with youth's indifference
the berries bright against the storm's grey ghost

Colour: Titanium White/ Music: *In the Bleak Midwinter, Harold Darke, words by Christina Rossetti*

Celtic goddesses vye for supremacy

Beira, queen of winter, stumbles through drifts of snow;
her failing lungs emitting a ghostly whistle

Gothic palaces loom   icicle daggers
glower from warped guttering...
Crows scavenge like hooded monks in murderous gaggles

On strangled branches spent leaves gasp their last
as storm winds drum with hollow sticks down muddy lanes.

Yet   feeling the nudge of a new pretender,
the weighted darts of rivalry,
she knows her time is up   yet resists,
struggles to surrender to Oestre's vernal embrace...

then   finally as green shoots pierce scumbled soil
and Oestre's magicke frees the earth from hibernation

she relinquishes the keys to her realm

Colour: Crimson/ Music: *Jan Gabarek Parce Mini Dominum from the Officium Novum album*) *(based on Officium Defunctorum by Cristóbal de Morales)*

Poppies in Giverny
Memories of visits to Monet's Garden

Much-tainted by words
of grief and remembrance for
those who served and fell,

the crimson swathes stand
tall by Monet's house, no grief
on view, just ploughshares.

Our mind's eye sees the
sacrifice and paints them red,
denying their truth.

Monet picks up his
brush, splashes watercolour
on canvas - et voilà! *Les coquelicots*

Colour: Gunmetal Grey/ Music: *Thomas Tallis Spem in Alium*

After Ragnarök *

Sough of wind at our backs
Sigh of rain-drenched foliage

Twilight approaching....
                    Götterdämmerung*

Lick of crimson-tongued flames
        presaging evil —
                dark infernos to come

Norse gods long submerged
            arise in a new world
                    exhaling fresh breath.

Earth finally cleansed!

They once trod this forest, their
heartbeats still palpable today   listen!

Water now rises around us   unstoppable
    Sintflut * *   World's End coming!

Which of us will survive?

 *Twilight of the gods (old Norse and German)
* * The great biblical flood

EPILOGUE

Nature versus Nurture

The great Aristotle once said
Give me a child until he is seven
And I will show you the man.

I ask myself which influence was greater.
Which factor most determined who I am?

Some say we are hot-wired before birth,
behaviour pre-ordained within the womb.

Yet others say it stems from different factors,
exposure, education and experience.

When I recall myself at seven years old
and try to weigh up what my markers were,

I reach the firm conclusion that
both nature and nurture shaped me equally.

My truth

Looking back now I wouldn't change a thing,
for no life lived is ever really charmed.
Each human has his challenges to face,
Leaving him wounded, pitted with deep scars.

Most parents do the best they can for us
but only have the skills that they once learnt.
We should applaud those efforts made with love ...
Our merits too as parents must be earned.

ACKNOWLEDGEMENTS

First and foremost a huge thank you to my publisher, Mark Davidson for supporting my poetic endeavours and agreeing to publish this latest poetry collection.

Thanks to all my Hoglet poetry buddies (too numerous to mention) and those on Twitter, Facebook and Instagram for their support and encouragement of my work via social media. A special shout out for Damien B Donnelly for his ongoing support with book launches, reviewing my work and tireless promotion of the poetry community via his podcasts and journals.

Thanks too to Patricia M Osborne, Phil Vernon and Dr Antje Bothin for reviews for the book jacket.

A big thank you to my dear friend, Marian Williamson, for her beautiful artwork done especially for the book and postcards.

Gratitude to the following journals, where the following poems were first published:

The Storms Journal 1 (editor Damien B Donnelly) for 'After Ragnarök'

Impspired Magazine (editor Steve Cawte) for ' Blackcurrant Wine', 'A love-hate relationship with my dark under-eye circles' 'The Blue Hour' ' Wolf Moon Haunts...(retitled here as Halloween)

Flights Journal (editors Darren J Beaney and Barbara Kirbyshaw) for 'The Swinging Sixties'

Hedgehog Press for 'A Postcard from Scarborough' in 'Wish you Were There', 'Villanelle for The First Men on the Moon'

Dreich Magazine (editor Jack Caradoc) for 'Spurn Point Lighthouse' in anthology ' At the Edge of All Storms'

Crumps Barn Studio for 'MJB' and 'Visiting my Great Aunts' (in my memoir *The Road to Cleethorpes Pier*)

Fevers of the Mind Showcase by David L O'Nan for 'The Black Hole of Calcutta' and 'My Nanna's sayings were pure gold'